Trish Deseine

Trifles

Photographs by Deirdre Rooney

HACHETTE
illustrated

contents

tricks of the trade

A little bit of history

The first recipe for this English pudding dates back to 1560. At that time, trifle was no more than cooked cream flavoured with orange flower water or ginger and decorated with preserved fruit. It did not acquire its now classic layered form until towards the end of the 18th century.

The sequence of layers is possibly the only rule to respect when making a trifle: sponge cake soaked in alcohol, followed by fruit, fruit compote or jam, custard and finished off with whipped cream. It is important that the layers merge slightly and that there is a contrast between the sweetness and tartness as well as between the different textures of the layers. The advantage of this dessert is that it makes itself while chilling quietly in the fridge. The longer you leave it alone, the better it will be.

Sponge base

The easiest option is to buy ready-made trifle sponges; they live up to their name, being so incredibly absorbent that you can pour in half a bottle of brandy before even thinking of the other layers. With their smooth texture, trifle sponges are equally good at soaking up the juices from fruit compote or from canned fruits in syrup.

Alternatively, you can use any sponge or Madeira cake, although they may be slightly heavy if made with a lot of butter. Sponge finger boudoir biscuits also make very good bases for trifles. Once you have grasped the principle, you can play around with brioche, amaretti, pains au chocolat, tea breads, muffins, meringues, or whatever takes your fancy.

Fruit and jelly

Red berry fruits are perfect for trifles. Cherries, raspberries and strawberries produce a lot of juice, acidity and colour, creating a pleasing contrast with the other sweeter layers. Gooseberries, apricots, plums, blackcurrants and rhubarb are also excellent. Fruits with less juice can be stewed lightly into a compote, or poached in syrup. The important thing is to balance the flavours of the layers to achieve the contrast.

The Great Jelly Debate rages on. Purists disdainfully dismiss it, fanatics cannot live without it. Personally, I feel jelly has earned its stripes along with hundreds-and-thousands and glacé cherries, if only as a nod to nostalgia. These recipes were first destined for my French readers, who, already finding it difficult to correctly pronounce 'Treifeul', would not have appreciated finding the elusive and much ridiculed substance on their ingredient lists. Do not believe, therefore, that it has been deliberately eliminated through unbearably self-righteous culinary snobbery and please feel free to reinstate it wherever you feel the wobbly urge.

Custard

The custard layer presents a problem for people who have not mastered the art of making homemade custard.

If this is the case with you, there are several ways of cheating – you can buy custard in powder form, to which you add sugar and milk and stir over gentle heat until thick or cartons of ready-made custard, some brands of which are excellent) and simply pour it over the fruit layer before topping with a layer of whipped cream.

Whipped cream and decoration

For the final layer, you can use either double cream, whipping cream supplemented with a little mascarpone cheese for extra richness, if you want, or syllabub. Syllabub is cream whipped with a little lemon juice and grated rind, brandy, white wine and sugar.

You can play around with this final layer using liqueurs flavoured with the fruits you have used for the inner layers; liqueurs such as cherry, blackberry, raspberry or apricot will really enhance the flavour of your trifle wonderfully.

Glacé cherries and whole or flaked toasted almonds are still the great classics in trifle decoration. There are also many nostalgic devotees of hundreds-and-thousands, which will add a touch of kitsch to this most English of puddings.

A few hours in the fridge…

To make a good trifle, leave it in the refrigerator for as long as possible: it will only improve.

Ideally, leave the trifle to chill for 1–2 hours between each layer. But the most important thing to remember is that most fully assembled trifles should chill in the refrigerator for 5–6 hours before serving; although some may need less time and the relevant recipes will indicate this. If you have time, I would recommend that you make it the previous evening and leave it to chill overnight.

It is very difficult to give precise quantities for trifle recipes. It all depends on the size and shape of the container you are using and the number you are feeding. The quantities given here, unless otherwise specified, are for a medium-sized trifle to serve 4–6 people generously, (and how else would you want to serve them?) made in a traditional trifle dish. When the trifle is to be served in individual dishes, with no chance of seconds, the quantities matter even less!

Real sherry trifle

Serves 4-6 very generously

6–8 trifle sponges

4–5 tablespoons cherry jam

4–5 tablespoons sherry, medium to sweet

about 10 amaretti biscuits

625–875 g (1¼–1¾ lb) cherry compote or pitted cherries in syrup

750 ml (¼ pints) vanilla custard (see recipe on page 8)

350 ml (12 fl oz) whipping cream

2 tablespoons caster sugar

toasted almonds, to decorate

Spread the trifle sponges with the cherry jam, then arrange them in the base of a trifle dish.

Sprinkle with sherry, pressing down lightly to ensure that the sherry permeates the sponge base thoroughly. Crush the amaretti biscuits and sprinkle over the sponge layer.

Add a layer of cherries, followed by a layer of custard.

Using an electric beater whip the cream with the sugar and spread over the custard layer.

Leave to chill in the refrigerator for at least 2-3 hours.

Just before serving, decorate the trifle with toasted almonds.

The St. John trifle

A recipe kindly supplied by Fergus Henderson from his unique London restaurant, where it is served as a shared dessert for two (a nerve-racking method for the truly greedy).

Serves 6

For the custard:

300 ml (½ pint) full-fat milk

300 ml (½ pint) whipping cream

1 vanilla pod, split in half

4 egg yolks

125 g (4 oz) caster sugar

For the sponge:

6 eggs, separated

350 g (12 oz) caster sugar

175 g (6 oz) plain flour

40 g (1½ oz) cornflour

icing sugar

For the cherry compote:

25 g (1 oz) sugar

450 g (15 oz) black cherries, pitted

4 tablespoons lemon juice

4–5 tablespoons Marsala wine or sherry

300 ml (½ pint) whipping cream

50 g (2 oz) toasted flaked almonds

For the custard, bring the milk, cream and vanilla pod to the boil in a pan. Meanwhile, beat the egg yolks with the sugar. Remove the vanilla pod and pour the hot liquid into the egg mixture, beating constantly. Return the mixture to the pan together with the vanilla pod and cook over gentle heat, stirring with a wooden spoon, until it thickens. Do not allow to boil. Pass the custard through a sieve and leave to cool.

To make the sponge, preheat the oven to 180ºC (350ºF), gas mark 4. Beat the egg yolks with half the sugar until pale and fluffy. In a separate bowl, whisk the egg whites to stiff peaks, then add the remaining sugar. Fold the egg whites into the yolk mixture. Sift the plain flour and cornflour together, then fold gently into the egg mixture in three batches. Spoon the mixture into a shallow baking tray lined with greaseproof paper, or in individual portions on a greased, lined baking sheet to make sponge fingers. Sprinkle with icing sugar and bake for about 15 minutes or until the sponge is pale and golden.

To make the compote, dissolve the sugar in a little water over low heat, add 125 g (4 oz) of the cherries and the lemon juice and poach gently for 10 minutes. Purée in a blender and, while still hot, stir into the remaining whole cherries. Leave to cool.

Spoon the cherry compote into individual dishes. Cut the sponge into pieces and place over the compote. Sprinkle with Marsala or sherry and chill for about 10 minutes. Pour the custard over the top and chill in the refrigerator overnight.

Just before serving, whip the cream into soft peaks, spoon over the custard and decorate with toasted almonds.

The Wolseley trifle

This stunning London restaurant, an overnight institution, has the skilful and passionate Claire Clark as its pastry chef. This is her recipe for an elegantly sculptural trifle.

Serves 10-12

3 eggs

475 g (15 oz) caster sugar

50 g (2 oz) plain flour

7 tablespoons cocoa powder

100 ml (3½ fl oz) water

100 ml (3½ fl oz) kirsch liqueur

500 g (1 lb) pitted black cherries in syrup

200 g (7 oz) good quality dark chocolate, broken into pieces

125 g (4 oz) white chocolate, broken into pieces

40 g (1½ oz) cornflour

500 ml (17 fl oz) whipped cream

dark chocolare curls, to decorate

For the sponge, preheat the oven to 180ºC (350ºF), gas mark 4. Beat the eggs with 75 g (3 oz) sugar. Sift the flour with 2 tablespoons of the cocoa powder, then fold into the beaten eggs. Spread a 1-cm (½-inch) layer of the mixture on a baking sheet lined with greaseproof paper and bake for 10 minutes.

Bring the measured water to the boil with 100 g (3½ oz) sugar, then add half the kirsch liqueur. Leave to cool. Cut the sponge into rounds to fit the serving glasses. Place the rounds in a large shallow dish and sprinkle with the cooled syrup. Leave to soak.

Bring the cherries to the boil in their juice with 50 g (2 oz) sugar. Dissolve half the cornflour in a little cold water and add to the cherries. Stir until it thickens, then simmer over a low heat for a further 2 minutes. Add the remaining kirsch and leave to cool.

Melt 125 g (4 oz) of the dark and all of the white chocolate in 2 separate bowls over pans of barely simmering water. Remove and leave to cool slightly. Divide the whipped cream between 2 bowls and fold melted chocolate into each to make 2 mousses.

For the sauce, bring 300 ml (½ pint) water almost to the boil with the remaining sugar and chocolate. Stir until both have melted. Mix the remaining cocoa powder and cornflour in a little cold water to a smooth paste, add the hot chocolate and whisk. Return to the heat and cook for 3 minutes. Leave to cool.

With an icing bag, pipe lines of mousse, alternating the colours, into the serving glasses. Build up alternate layers of sponge and cherry compote, top with a layer of mousse, pour over the chocolate sauce and decorate with whipped cream. Refrigerate for 5-6 hours and serve decorated with dark chocolate curls.

Fruit jelly

Serves 4

250 ml (8 fl oz) water

1 packet raspberry jelly

250 ml (8 fl oz) red wine

150 g (5 oz) strawberries (halved if they are big)

125 g (4 oz) raspberries

crème fraîche, Greek yogurt or whipped cream, to serve

Bring the measured water to the boil. Cut the jelly into cubes and place in a heatproof bowl, pour over the water and stir until dissolved. Add the wine and leave to cool slightly.

Stir the fruit into the liquid jelly, then pour into individual glasses. Place in the refrigerator for 1-2 hours to set.

Serve with crème fraîche, Greek yogurt or whipped cream.

Variation | Instead of raspberry jelly and red wine, use a lemon jelly and a sweet dessert white wine, such as Beaumes de Venise, and sliced apple and white grapes instead of red berry fruits.

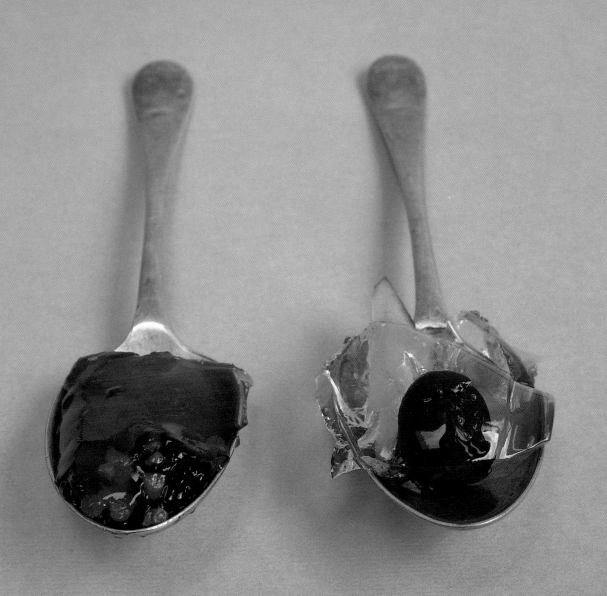

Cheats' trifle

Serves 4-6

**1 packet trifle sponges
or sponge finger boudoir
biscuits**

**4 tablespoons Marsala wine
or brandy**

**300 g (10 oz) jar cherry
compote**

**250 ml (8 fl oz) whipping
cream**

**150 ml (¼ pint) ready-made
custard**

**2 tablespoons caster sugar,
or to taste**

**hundreds-and-thousands
or toasted almonds, to
decorate**

Arrange the sponges over the base of the dish, sprinkle with the Marsala or brandy and cover with the cherry compote.

Whip the cream into peaks, stir in the ready-made custard, and sugar to taste.

Spread the custard cream over the compote and leave to chill in the refrigerator for 4-5 hours.

Decorate with hundreds-and-thousands or toasted almonds before serving. If you are feeling particularly indulgent, you can also top with an extra layer of whipped cream.

Banana and strawberry trifle

Serves 4-6

about 15 sponge finger
boudoir biscuits or 6 trifle
sponges

4–5 tablespoons sherry
or Marsala (or freshly
squeezed orange juice
for children!)

2 bananas

2 tablespoons lemon juice

200 g (7 oz) strawberries

750 ml (1¼ pints) vanilla
custard (see recipe on
page 8)

350 ml (12 fl oz) whipping
cream

2 tablespoons caster sugar

hundreds-and-thousands,
to decorate

Arrange the sponge fingers over the base of a trifle dish.
Sprinkle with the sherry, Marsala or orange juice, and press
down lightly so that the liquid permeates the sponge
thoroughly.

Slice the bananas and toss in the lemon juice to prevent
discoloration. Halve the strawberries.

Arrange slices of bananas and strawberries against the inside
of the trifle dish, then mix the remaining fruit together and
use it to fill the centre. Pour the custard over the fruit.

Using an electric beater, whip the cream with the sugar and
spread over the custard layer. Leave to chill in the refrigerator
for 5-6 hours.

Decorate with hundreds-and-thousands just before serving.

Black Forest trifle

Serves 6

6 eggs, separated

200 g (7 oz) caster sugar

40 g (1½ oz) cocoa powder

1 jar Morello cherries in kirsch

300 ml (½ pint) whipping cream

caster sugar, to taste, optional

100 g (3½ oz) good quality dark chocolate

100 g (3½ oz) dark chocolate curls, to decorate

Preheat the oven to 180ºC (350ºF), gas mark 4.

Grease and line a 24-cm (10-inch) diameter, deep cake tin.

To make the chocolate sponge, beat the egg yolks with the 200 g (7 oz) sugar until the mixture is pale and fluffy. Carefully fold in the cocoa powder. Whisk the egg whites into stiff peaks and carefully fold into the chocolate mixture in three batches so that the egg whites do not collapse. Transfer to the cake tin and bake for about 20 minutes. The top of the cake should be soft to the touch.

Leave the cake to cool slightly in the tin on a wire rack, then turn out and leave to cool completely.

Drain the cherries, reserving the syrup.

Using an electric beater, whip the cream into peaks with caster sugar to taste, if required. Cut the cake into two layers and place one layer on the base of a serving dish. Pour half of the cherry syrup over the sponge cake and top with half of the cherries. Spread over half the whipped cream.

Melt the chocolate in a microwave oven or in a bowl placed over a pan of barely simmering water.

Using a spatula, spread a thin layer of melted chocolate as evenly as possible on the underside of the second half of the cake and place on top of the trifle. Pour over the remaining syrup, scatter the remaining cherries (reserving a few for decoration) and spread over the rest of the whipped cream. Decorate with the cherries and chocolate curls.

Leave to chill in the refrigerator for a minimum of 2 hours before serving.

Pink rhubarb and white chocolate trifle

Serves 6-8

500 ml (17 fl oz) whipping cream

150 g (5 oz) good quality white chocolate, broken into small pieces

6–7 sticks of rhubarb, peeled and cut into chunks or 250 g (8 oz) frozen rhubarb

3–4 tablespoons caster sugar

1 packet sponge finger boudoir biscuits

Bring the cream almost to the boil and pour over the white chocolate. Stir until the chocolate has completely melted, then place in the refrigerator for at least 2 hours. It must be very cold or it will not whip properly.

Poach the rhubarb over low heat with a little water to prevent it sticking as it starts to cook. Add a little sugar, but not too much: the tartness of the fruit should be in stark contrast to the chocolate mousse. The rhubarb must be very soft.

Whip the chocolate cream.

Line the base of the serving bowl with the boudoir biscuits, leaving aside a few for decoration, if desired. Add the rhubarb and cover with a layer of chocolate cream. Repeat the process once or twice, depending on the shape of your bowl.

Return the trifle to the refrigerator and leave for at least 2 hours for the flavours to blend and the boudoir biscuits to soften on contact with the rhubarb juices.

Crumble the reserved sponge finger biscuits over the top to decorate, if you wish.

Death by chocolate trifle

Serves 4-6

4 medium-sized chocolate muffins (preferably with chocolate chips)

6–7 tablespoons Kahlua or other coffee liqueur

350 ml (12 fl oz) whipping cream

150 g (5 oz) good quality dark chocolate, broken into pieces

chocolate nibbles or dark chocolate curls, to decorate

Crumble the muffins into a serving bowl, pour over the coffee liqueur, and place in the refrigerator.

Bring the cream almost to the boil, remove from the heat, add the chocolate and stir to melt. Leave to cool, then pour over the muffin layer. Leave to chill in the refrigerator overnight.

Decorate with crunchy chocolate nibbles, or simply with curls of dark chocolate.

Mocha trifle

Serves 4

500 ml (17 fl oz) whipping cream

75 g (3 oz) dark chocolate 'coffee beans' or coffee flavoured chocolate

2 espresso-sized cups of espresso coffee

4 tablespoons Tia Maria or other coffee liqueur

1 small chocolate sponge cake or 4 medium-sized chocolate muffins

2 tablespoons caster sugar

In a large saucepan, bring 200 ml (7 fl oz) of the cream almost to the boil. Remove from the heat, add the chocolate 'coffee beans' and stir until completely melted and the mixture is smooth and creamy. Leave to cool slightly.

Make the espresso coffee and leave to cool. Stir in the coffee liqueur.

Break up the sponge cake or muffins and arrange in the base of the serving dish. Sprinkle with the coffee and liqueur mixture. Spread over a layer of the chocolate cream.

Using an electric beater, whip the remaining cream into peaks with the sugar, and spread over the chocolate cream layer.

Leave to chill in the refrigerator for 4-5 hours.

Not-really-a-trifle trifle with profiteroles

Serves 4

12–15 cream-and-chocolate filled profiteroles

350 ml (12 fl oz) whipping cream

5–6 tablespoons Baileys Irish Cream liqueur

150 g (5 oz) good quality dark chocolate, grated

Cut the profiteroles in half and arrange in the base of individual serving dishes.

Using an electric beater whip the cream into peaks.

Sprinkle the profiteroles with the Baileys, then top with the whipped cream.

Chill for 30 minutes at the most (here we bend the rule about the absorbent layer in favour of the law of sheer greed). Decorate with the grated chocolate and serve immediately.

Breakfast trifle

Serves 4

fresh fruit, such as grapes, bananas, strawberries or raspberries, depending on the season

6–8 tablespoons muesli or a mixture of your favourite cereals

2 small pots strawberry or raspberry yogurt

Cut the fruit into thin slices.

Fill individual glasses with alternating layers of cereal and fruit.

Pour the yogurt over the fruit just before serving.

Tea and orange trifle

Serves 4

1 espresso-size cup of
strong Earl Grey tea

1 small fresh brioche loaf,
sliced

4 small oranges, peeled
and quartered (reserve any
juice)

grated rind of 1 orange

500 ml (17 fl oz) whipping
cream

2 tablespoons caster sugar

a few kumquats, to decorate

Make the tea and leave to cool.

Arrange the brioche slices over the base of the serving bowl.

Remove all the pith and membrane from the orange quarters
and scatter over the brioche along with the grated rind and
any juice.

Using an electric beater, whip the cream into peaks, stir in the
tea and sugar, then spread over the oranges.

Leave to chill in the refrigerator for 4-5 hours. Decorate with
slices of kumquat before serving.

Rum and raisin trifle

Serves 4

200 ml (7 fl oz) rum

100 g (3½ oz) sultanas

350 ml (12 fl oz) whipping cream

2 tablespoons caster sugar

1 small fruit loaf

1 fresh pineapple, peeled and cut into bite-sized chunks

750 ml (1¼ pints) vanilla custard (see recipe on page 8)

soft brown or muscovado sugar, to decorate

Heat the rum and the sultanas in a saucepan, flambéing them if you wish (watch your eyebrows!). Remove the pan from the heat and leave to cool. The sultanas will swell.

Using an electric beater, whip the cream into peaks along with the sugar.

Cut the fruit loaf into slices and arrange over the base of the trifle dish. Scatter the sultanas together with any remaining rum over the fruit loaf, adding extra rum if you wish, followed by the pineapple chunks.

Cover with a layer of custard and top with the whipped cream. Leave to chill in the refrigerator for 4-5 hours.

Decorate with a sprinkling of soft brown or muscovado sugar.

Trifle with almonds, strawberries, pistachio nuts and orange flower water

Serves 4

6–8 almond shortbread biscuits or any other small almond biscuits

150 g (5 oz) strawberries, halved or quartered if large

30 g (1 oz) blanched almonds, chopped

500 ml (17 fl oz) whipping cream

1 tablespoon orange flower water

30 g (1 oz) unsalted green pistachio nuts

2 tablespoons caster sugar

a few pieces of Turkish delight, to decorate

Crumble the biscuits into the base of the serving glasses.

Arrange the strawberries over the biscuits and leave to soak up the juices.

Toast the almonds in a dry frying pan.

Whip the cream and stir in the orange flower water, pistachio nuts, almonds and sugar. Spread the cream mixture over the biscuit and strawberry layer and leave to chill in the refrigerator for at least 2 hours.

Decorate with small pieces of Turkish delight before serving.

Banoffee trifle

Serves 4

80 g (3 oz) butter

4 bananas

about 10 chocolate digestive biscuits

350 ml (12 fl oz) whipping cream

1–2 tablespoons caster sugar

1 pot Dulce de Leche, or 1 can sweetened condensed milk

If using condensed milk, empty the contents into a large microwave-safe bowl and microwave on medium power for 2 minutes. Stir with a whisk, then microwave on medium power for another 2 minutes. Stir again and return to the microwave for 15-25 minutes on medium-low power or until the milk thickens and turns caramel in colour, stirring every few minutes. Be careful, this will get very hot. Leave to cool completely.

Melt the butter and leave to cool.

Using a rolling pin, crush the biscuits in a clean tea towel and add to the melted butter.

Slice the bananas.

Using an electric beater whip the cream into peaks along with the sugar.

Assemble the trifle in a serving bowl or in individual glass bowls, alternating layers of biscuit crumbs, sliced bananas, caramel sauce and whipped cream, and serve immediately.

Mont Blanc trifle

Serves 4

About 10 sponge finger boudoir biscuits

6–8 tablespoons dark rum

6–8 tablespoons sweet chestnut purée

500 g (1 lb) crème fraîche

Crumble the sponge fingers into the base of individual stemmed glasses, sprinkle with the rum and chill.

Add a layer of chestnut purée followed by a thick layer of crème fraîche. Its slightly tart flavour will complement the extremely sweet chestnut purée perfectly.

Leave the trifles to chill in the refrigerator for 4 hours.

Peach, Sauternes and vanilla trifle

Serves 4-6

5–6 slices fresh brioche

4–5 tablespoons sweet white wine, such as Sauternes

500 g (1 lb) canned peaches in syrup

350 ml (12 fl oz) whipping cream

2 tablespoons caster sugar

500 ml (17 fl oz) custard made with a whole vanilla pod (see recipe on page 8)

Arrange the brioche slices in the base of a large serving bowl. Sprinkle with the wine and press lightly so that the wine permeates the brioche thoroughly.

Drain the peaches and arrange on the brioche layer.

Using an electric beater, whip the cream into peaks along with the sugar. Fold the custard into the cream.

Pour this mixture over the peaches and leave to chill in the refrigerator for 5-6 hours.

Black and blue trifle

Serves 4-6

about 10 sponge finger
boudoir biscuits

1 packet blackcurrant jelly,
cut into cubes

300 g (10 oz) mixed
blackberries, blackcurrants
and blueberries

300 ml (½ pint) whipping
cream

caster sugar, to taste

Break the sponge finger biscuits into pieces and arrange in the base of the trifle dish.

Dissolve the jelly cubes in hot water, following the instructions on the packet.

Pour a layer of jelly over the sponge finger pieces and chill to set slightly. Add the fruit to the remaining jelly and pour into the trifle dish. Leave to chill in the refrigerator for at least 3 hours.

Whip the cream with sugar, to taste, and spread over the top of the set jelly.

Tip | You can also add a layer of custard beneath the whipped cream.

Deconstructed trifle

Serves 4

1 Madeira cake, cut into slices

juice of 2 oranges

4 tablespoons Grand Marnier

1 pineapple, peeled and cut into chunks

1 mango, peeled and diced

flesh of 4 passion fruit

250 ml (8 fl oz) whipping cream

1–2 tablespoons caster sugar

Arrange the slices of cake on dessert plates. (The cake is also delicious toasted.)

Combine the orange juice with the Grand Marnier. Stir in all the fruit, then spoon this mixture over, or to the side of, the slices of cake.

Using an electric beater whip the cream into peaks along with the sugar.

Spoon the cream mixture over the cake and fruit and serve immediately.

Gooseberry trifle

Serves 6-8

1 small Madeira cake,
cut into slices, or 4–6 trifle
sponges, or about
15 sponge finger boudoir
biscuits

4–5 tablespoons sherry,
brandy, or Marsala wine

600–800 g (1¼–1¾ lb)
gooseberry compote

750 ml (1¼ pints) vanilla
custard (see recipe on
page 8)

750 ml (1¼ pints) whipping
cream

2 tablespoons caster sugar

white or red currants, to
decorate

Arrange the slices of cake or the sponge fingers in the base of a trifle dish.

Sprinkle with the alcohol and press down lightly so that it permeates the sponge thoroughly.

Add a layer of gooseberry compote followed by a layer of custard. Using an electric beater, whip the cream with the sugar, and spread over the custard layer. Leave to chill in the refrigerator for 5-6 hours.

Just before serving, decorate with white or red currants or any other attractive fruit you fancy.

Ginger syllabub trifle

Serves 4

4 slices gingerbread

2 tablespoons stem ginger, finely diced

8 tablespoons Syllabub (see recipe on page 56)

pared rind of 1 lemon

Crumble the gingerbread slices into the base of individual glasses or a large trifle dish.

Scatter the stem ginger over the gingerbread.

Cover with the Syllabub and leave to chill in the refrigerator for 4-5 hours.

Decorate with strips of lemon rind.

Apple and maple syrup trifle

Serves 4

6–8 digestive biscuits

300 ml (½ pint) whipping cream

3–4 tablespoons maple syrup

2 Granny Smith apples

lemon juice

Crush the biscuits and place a layer at the base of four glasses. Using an electric beater, whip the cream into peaks and stir in the maple syrup.

Pour half the cream mixture over the layer of crushed biscuits, add a layer of the remaining crushed biscuits followed by the rest of the cream. Chill in the refrigerator for a minimum of 1-2 hours.

Just before serving, core the apples and cut into thin slices. Cut the slices into strips, sprinkle with the lemon juice to prevent any discoloration and scatter over the top of the trifles.

Jam Swiss roll trifle

Serves 4

2 jam Swiss rolls, cut into slices

4–5 tablespoons Marsala wine

300 g (10 oz) white and red seedless grapes, halved

750 ml (1¼ pints) custard

350 ml (12 fl oz) whipping cream

2 tablespoons caster sugar

glacé cherries, toasted almonds or halved grapes, to decorate

Arrange the Swiss roll slices in the base of the trifle dish. Sprinkle with Marsala and press down lightly so that the wine permeates the sponge thoroughly.

Cut the grapes in half and arrange over the sponge layer. Pour on the custard.

Using an electric beater, whip the cream into peaks with the sugar and spread over the custard layer. Leave to chill in the refrigerator for 4-5 hours.

Decorate with glacé cherries, toasted almonds or halved grapes just before serving.

Cranachan

Serves 4

100 g (3½ oz) rolled oats

500 ml (17 fl oz) double cream

2 tablespoons caster sugar

3–4 tablespoons Scotch whisky

250 g (8 oz) raspberries

Preheat the oven to 180ºC (350ºF), gas mark 4 and roast the rolled oats until they are beautifully golden.

Using an electric beater, whip the cream into peaks with the sugar and stir in the whisky.

In individual glasses, place alternate layers of raspberries, rolled oats and the whisky cream.

Leave to chill in the refrigerator for 2-3 hours before serving.

Syllabub

Pour 4 à 6 personnes

Finely grated rind and juice of 3 lemons

4 tablespoons brandy

4–5 tablespoons caster sugar

400 ml (14 fl oz) double cream

almond biscuits, to serve

Place the lemon rind and juice, brandy and sugar in a large mixing bowl. Using an electric beater, add in the cream a little at a time, whisking constantly until it stands in peaks.

Spoon into individual glasses and leave to chill in the refrigerator for 3-4 hours.

Serve with almond biscuits.

Prune and Armagnac fool

Fools are desserts made with puréed fresh or stewed fruit that is then folded into whipped cream to create a marbled effect. Most fruits are suitable. You can also use several fruits at a time and add liqueurs to the purée.

Serves 4

about 15 pitted prunes

2–3 tablespoons Armagnac

500 ml (17 fl oz) whipping cream

2 tablespoons caster sugar

Place the prunes in a blender and whizz into a purée. Stir in the Armagnac.

Using an electric beater, whip the cream along with the sugar. Carefully fold the fruit purée into the cream to create an attractive marbled effect.

Chill in the refrigerator for at least 2 hours before serving.

Eton mess

Serves 6

250 ml (8 fl oz) whipping cream

2–3 tablespoons caster sugar

500 g (1 lb) raspberries

kirsch (optional)

For homemade meringues:

5 egg whites

250 g (8 oz) caster sugar

To make the meringues, preheat the oven to 120ºC (250ºF), gas mark 1/2.

Whisk the egg whites using an electric beater. When they start to form soft peaks, add the sugar, a spoonful at a time, beating after each addition. When the meringue mixture forms stiff peaks and is glossy, spoon small mounds onto a baking sheet lined with greaseproof paper and bake for about 50 minutes. Remove from the oven and leave to cool on the baking sheet. When quite cold, break into pieces.

To make 'the mess', whip the cream with the sugar using an electric beater.

Crush about half of the raspberries and stir in to the whole ones together with some sugar to taste and a little kirsch, if using.

Put the meringue pieces, whipped cream and the raspberries into a large bowl and gently stir into a lovely, great mess. Place in the refrigerator to chill for an hour or two before serving.

Tip | If you are in a hurry, use store-bought meringues for this recipe.

Veiled maidens

A beautifully evocative, if rather curious, name for this Scandinavian take on trifle.

Serves 4

4–5 cooking apples, peeled and cored

6 tablespoons caster sugar

50 g (2 oz) unsalted butter

about 10 digestive biscuits

350 ml (12 fl oz) whipping cream

toasted almonds, to decorate (optional)

Cut the apples into pieces and stew with 2 tablespoons of the sugar (or more, if they are very tart). When they are soft, purée or finely mash them, and leave to cool.

Melt the butter. Crush the biscuits and combine the crumbs with the butter. Add 2 tablespoons of caster sugar and mix together well.

Using an electric beater, whip the cream with the remaining 2 tablespoons of sugar.

In the base of a large trifle dish or individual glasses, place a layer of the biscuit mixture, followed by a layer of apple purée and a layer of the whipped cream. Repeat once more. Chill thoroughly and decorate with biscuit crumbs or toasted almonds just before serving.

Acknowledgements

Claire Clark and Helen Smith from The Wolseley.
The Wolseley | 160 Piccadilly | London | W15 9EB |
tel. +44 (0) 207 251 0848

Fergus Henderson and the charming staff from
St John. Please may I come back?
St John | 26 St John Street| London | EC1M 4AY|
tel. +44 (0) 207 251 0848

The Dining Room shop in Barnes.

My agent, Ivan Mulcahy. This is a mere trifle, perhaps,
but pudding for starters is always fine by me.

Margo Stevens and her drawers.

Shopping

Luminarc: pages 7, 53.

Dining Room Shop: pages 13, 21, 45, 57.

David Mellor: pages 15, 23, 29, 39, 61.

Jasper Conran for Wedgwood: pages 19, 37.

Bodum: pages 21, 51, 55, 63.

DaDriade: page 25, cup on page 31.

Habitat: plate on page 15, pages 23, 59.

Crate and Barrel: page 27.

Kitchen Bazaar: spoon on page 31.

Addresses

The Dining Room Shop
62-64 White Hart Lane, Barnes, London SW13 OPZ
www.thediningroomshop.co.uk

DaDriade
Via Manzoni, 20121 Milano, Italy
tel. +39 02 760 23098
info@dadriade.it

Crate and Barrel
650 Madison Ave, New York NY 10022, USA
tel. +1 212 308 0011

David Mellor
4 Sloane Square, London SW1 8EE
davidmellor@ukonline.co.uk

Kitchen Bazaar
23 bd de la Madeleine, 75001 Paris, France
tel. 01 42 60 50 30
www.kitchenbazaar.fr

The Conran Shop
12 Conduit Street, London W1S 2XQ
tel. +44 (0)20 7399 0710

This edition © Marabout 2004
This edition published by Hachette Illustrated UK, Octopus Publishing Group Ltd.,
2–4 Heron Quays, London E14 4JP

English translation by JMS Books LLP (email: Janem030@aol.com)
Translation © Octopus Publishing Group Ltd.

A CIP catalogue for this book is available from the British Library

ISBN 10: 1 84430 133 8

ISBN 13: 978 1 84430 133 1

Printed by Toppan Printing Co., (HK) Ltd.